ABOUT THE AUTHOR

Roger Sainsbury has over fifty years' experience of working in some of the most socially deprived communities in the United Kingdom, beginning in Spitalfields which was described in 1960 in the News of the World as 'the worst slum in Europe'.

His experience of church youth work in Spitalfields was followed by his appointment as Senior Youth Worker/Missioner at Shrewsbury House Youth Club in Liverpool. There he was one of the founders of West Everton Community Council which gave him his first experience of local politics.

His political experience grew when as Warden of the Mayflower Family Centre in Canning Town he was elected as an Alderman in the London Borough of Newham. As Alderman one of his main responsibilities was to Chair the Newham/Tower Hamlets Job Creation Committee. In 1980 he was appointed Rector of St. Matthew's Walsall, a large flourishing church in the West Midlands and was elected to the General Synod of the Church of England.

His experience in Walsall led to his appointment as Archdeacon of West Ham followed three years later by his consecration in St. Paul's Cathedral as Bishop of Barking which had an Episcopal Area of over one million people. As bishop he had a priority for urban evangelism and the involvement of churches with young people. During his time as Bishop of Barking he was also Chair of the Anglican Urban Bishops Panel, Chair of the Evangelical Coalition for Urban Mission, Moderator of the Churches Commission for Racial Justice and Chair of the London Churches Group for Social Action.

When he retired as Bishop of Barking he was invited in 2001 to become Chair of The National Youth Agency and later to Chair the Churches Together in England Urban Affairs Group. His involvement in grassroots youth work continued in Portishead, one of the fastest growing towns in the UK, where he was closely involved in the redevelopment of a £1M new youth centre.

Ten Commandments for
Today

Also by Bishop Roger Sainsbury

From a Mersey Wall	(Scripture Union, 1970)
Justice on the Agenda	(Marshalls, 1985)
Lifestyle	(Scripture Union, 1986)
God of New Beginnings	(Scripture Union, 1991)
Young People as Prophets	(Grove Books, 2006)

Bishop Roger Sainsbury

Ten Commandments for Today

Olympia Publishers
London

www.olympiapublishers.com
OLYMPIA PAPERBACK EDITION

A CIP catalogue record for this title is
available from the British Library.

ISBN: 978-1-84897-320-6

(Olympia Publishers is part of Ashwell Publishing Ltd)

First Published in 2013

Olympia Publishers
60 Cannon Street
London
EC4N 6NP

Printed in Great Britain

ACKNOWLEDGEMENTS

I would like to thank all those who have made this book possible.

Particularly Kimberley Dodd, from Portishead Youth Centre, who typed the manuscript, Staff at Frontier Youth Trust, Centre for Youth Ministry and The National Youth Agency, Michael Eastman, Editor of the Christian Coalition For Urban Mission magazine – Urban Bulletin and friends, clergy, fellow bishops and youth workers from my fifty years of urban ministry in East London, Liverpool, Walsall and Portishead.

I realize that there is some unevenness, repetition, and dateable material in the book that comes from the way it has been written. It is a book to be dipped into rather than read from cover to cover. If the book makes some small contribution to the very important debates taking place in the Church and society at the moment I shall be very grateful.

Roger F. Sainsbury
Portishead

CONTENTS

APPENDICES

INTRODUCTION

Martin Percy in the bible study notes my wife Jenny and I use in our daily prayers comments on the Ten Commandments in the bible – 'These are a core curriculum for human flourishing' (see Appendix 1).

During the 50 years of my ministry I have had a concern for the human flourishing of young people and have challenged those issues like cuts in youth services and youth unemployment that have had a negative impact on their flourishing.

Beginning my ministry in the shadow of the City of London in a community described in 1960 as the worst slum in Europe, I have long had real concern about the issues the Occupy London protesters have highlighted that spoil the human flourishing of many who live in the poorer communities in the U.K.

As an Anglican bishop since 2001 I have had the opportunity of visiting cities in Africa, Asia, Europe and America and have seen at first hand the challenge the Anglican churches were facing with over 50% of the world's population now living in cities. I believe the human flourishing of all those who live in those cities should be a top priority for the Anglican Communion.

When I was Chairman of The National Youth Agency I had a particular concern for the human flourishing of young people of different faiths (see Appendix 4).

As Moderator of the Church's Commission for Racial Justice, the human flourishing of Asylum Seekers and Immigrants was a major issue for me as was the welfare of our poorest citizens, during the whole of my ministry.

Now in 2013 Immigration and Welfare Benefits are at the top of the political agenda as we move towards the 2015 General Election.

All of us were encouraged by the human flourishing of young people during the 2012 Olympics and I agree with Maggie Atkinson the Children's Commissioner – 'Our young Olympians can inspire every generation' (Children and Young People Now, August 2012). As a student I worked at Stoke Mandeville Hospital where the Paralympics all began and therefore I was also particularly thrilled to see the human flourishing of everyone taking part in the Paralympic Games 2012.

I hope the following Ten Commandments may make a small contribution to the core curriculum for all those concerned today for human flourishing. It is fascinating that Alan de Botton in his popular book, 'Religion for Atheists' mentions the biblical Ten Commandments in a positive way as 'a first attempt at reining in man's aggression towards his fellow man (pg 84). A Guardian editorial (March 2013) spoke of the need for 'laws and principles' in the current debates about immigration. Perhaps these Ten Commandments may assist in meeting that need, not only in debates about immigration but in debates and decision making on a whole variety of issues we face as churches and society today.

BACKGROUND

My involvement in youth work began in 1958 as a volunteer in Portishead Nautical Approved School. After ordination in 1960, I ran a church youth club in Spitalfields. This was followed by eleven years in Shrewsbury House Youth Centre in Liverpool and seven years at the Mayflower Family Centre in East London. As Rector of Walsall and then Bishop of Barking, I supported a number of exciting youth projects and was involved in lobbying various Government Ministers (both Conservative and Labour) about the future of the youth service. As a result of this political involvement, I was invited to Chair the National Youth Agency in 2001. So that I knew at first hand what was happening at a grass roots level, on returning to Portishead, I was involved in the redevelopment of Portishead Youth Centre. One of the highlights of my time as Chair of The National Youth Agency was a two day Youth Summit Conference in 2007 which led to the Youth Summit Ten Commandments which I believe both from local and national experience are still very relevant today.

Responses from Portishead youth workers

Alan
"After forty years, I continue to be amazed at the value of good youth work."

Nadia
"My top three are two, three, and four. These are so important to establish good youth work in a youth work setting, so young people feel their views are respected"

Kim
"Commandment ten is the most important for me – getting young people to feel a part of their local community and for the local community to accept them is key to breaking down the national stereotypes associated with young people"

Hayley
"Four is important for me. Involve young people in decision making at every level and give RESPECT to their views. I feel that giving them the respect even though their views may not be correct is important – it is important to understand where they are coming from"

Charlie
"Local Councillors must listen to the voices of young people" (see Appendix 2).

Response from Jane Corbett

Shrewsbury House and Liverpool City Councillor (Cabinet Member for Children and Young People's Services

"If there is one thing that we need to ensure during this time is that our young people feel valued, respected and listened to... their voices must be heard if our society is to remain strong or we will reap the whirlwind in the very near future."

YOUTH SUMMIT TEN COMMANDMENTS

1. Do not demonise or use young people as scapegoats for the social ills of society.

2. Do not be afraid of speaking out about the value of good youth work.

3. Establish entitlement for all young people to good quality youth services.

4. Involve young people in decision making at every level and give respect to their views.

5. Campaign both locally and nationally for sustained and sufficient services for young people.

6. Create youth centres/hubs in each community with access in respect of transport, physical access, equality and diversity.

7. Work together with other public services to encourage young people to choose health.

8. Campaign for a defined programme of continuing professional development to increase the skills of all who work with young people and promote better multi-disciplinary working.

9. Recognise the right of all young people to locally accessible, free, confidential and impartial information, advice, counselling and support.

10. Encourage and enable young people to participate in building peaceful societies based on human rights, diversity and inclusion, in a spirit of respect, tolerance and mutual understanding.

Bishop Roger Sainsbury

Chair, the National Youth Agency 2001 – 2008 (The National Youth Agency, annual report 2006 – 2007)

BACKGROUND

In 1964 along with the late David Sheppard the former England Cricket Captain and Bishop of Liverpool, I was one of the founding members of Frontier Youth Trust which was then part of Scripture Union. Our concern was with what we called Open Christian Youth Work, with a focus on young people who never came near a church door. One of our priorities was to listen to the voices of young people and I did this sitting on a wall in Everton and put my thinking into a book published by Scripture Union called 'From a Mersey Wall'.

One of our concerns at Frontier Youth Trust along with other Christian Youth Work Agencies was that Christian Youth Workers should be professionally trained. As a result of this concern we came together at the Centre for Youth Ministry and for three years I had the privilege of chairing the Executive Committee. It was at one of these committee meetings that I wrote 'Ten Commandments for Youth Work Today'.

COMMENTS

Nigel Pimlott (Youth Work after Christendom)
"These not only provide extremely valuable signposts for effective youth work, they also focus upon the need for clear values and effective processes to underpin, inform, inspire and facilitate work with young people."

Dave Wiles (Kite Flying Consultancy 2012)
"Young people are human beings and not human becomings! They have been demonised, stigmatised, ignored and ostracised beyond belief! Youth and community services have been decimated to a point of nearly no return and the UK is storing up a back lash of gargantuan proportion for itself. The rhetoric about investing in the next generation from the recent Olympic Games must become a living reality across society if we want harmony between generations and within communities. These commandments are a great starting turning the tide – but remember they are commandments NOT suggestions! Ignore them at your peril! Shalom/Salaam/Pax".

Alistair Jones (Chief Executive of FYT 2012)
"I found they reminded me to root my youth work in my values of both informal education and my Christian faith. Calling me to the socially excluded and disadvantaged while at the same time encouraging young people in their significance and value while at the same time challenging those voices who are fast to criticise young people and slow to praise and acknowledge their achievements".

Kevin Davis (Vine Trust Walsall)
"We need positively to promote young people in order to change the negative perception of the young".

Pip Wilson (Mayflower Family Centre and YMCA)
"It costs to love young people – because love isn't a plaque you hang on a wall, it is something you *do* to young people".

TEN COMMANDMENTS FOR YOUTH WORK TODAY

1. Listen to the voices of young people.

2. Have a special concern for the socially excluded and disadvantaged.

3. Work co-operatively with other agencies, particularly schools.

4. Give spiritual development a priority.

5. Demonstrate tough love.

6. Offer emotional and spiritual security.

7. Organize activities that help young people feel valued and significant.

8. Challenge the demonization of young people.

9. Help build community cohesion by youth work that educates young people to value our common humanity and shared citizenship, not sectarian hate.

10. Be active politically to seek long-term funding for youth work from national and local government.

Bishop Roger Sainsbury
Centre for Youth Ministry 2008

BACKGROUND

The background to these Ten Commandments is an article I wrote in the Urban Bulletin [Issue 21] and the church report 'The lies we tell ourselves' (2013) which was seen as a response to the Government's far reaching welfare cuts.

SEEKING THE WELFARE OF OUR CITIES

'In our current political climate the word 'welfare' has almost become a dirty word.

'Seek the welfare of the City where I have sent you' is a biblical text from Jeremiah 29.7 that has been at the heart of my ministry for 50 years. This text was given added importance by our Evangelical Coalitition for Urban Mission 'Manifesto for Urban Mission' which stated clearly 'the welfare of our cities includes our social, economic and political situation.' Walter Brueggeman in his commentary on Jeremiah says this on the text-'such a horizon prevents the community from withdrawing into its own safe, sectarian existence, and gives it work to do and responsibility for the wider community.'

My 50 years of involvement in the issues of urban mission began as a volunteer in an approved school in Portishead, the town where I now live. I saw very clearly that many of the boys in the school came from very socially deprived backgrounds in our big cities and that had led them directly into crime. This experience in Portishead was repeated 20 years later in Canning

Town where I saw socially deprivation , particularly youth unemployment, was a breeding ground for youth crime [see story of Terry Smith in Appendix 6 on Gang, Gun and Knife Crime] .

Social deprivation for some in our cities does not lead into crime but through broken families into depression and mental illness. Such was the experience of a young girl in Shrewsbury House Youth Club in Liverpool in the 1960s. Although she came to a personal faith in Jesus Christ the big social issues from her background still needed addressing. Last month I saw her in her new home and was thrilled to see how over 40 years she had become a whole lovely person contributing in positive ways to her local community. She had received help from a whole variety of people and agencies during those years including State Welfare Benefits!!!!'

'The systematic misrepresentation of the poorest in society is a matter of injustice which all Christians have a responsibility to challenge. The myths challenged are not a comprehensive list but were chosen because of their prominence in public debate today.

- Myth 1: 'They' are lazy and just don't want to work

- Myth 2: 'They' are addicted to drink and drugs

- Myth 3: 'They' are not really poor – they just don't manage their money properly

- Myth 4: 'They' are on the fiddle

- Myth 5: 'They' have an easy life on benefits

- Myth 6: 'They' caused the deficit'

WELFARE TEN COMMANDMENTS

1. Seeking the Welfare of our Cities [Jeremiah 29.7] and all who live there should be a first priority for Governments and Churches.

2. Welfare is an attack on Want [Beveridge].

3. Welfare must include the social, economic and political situation of all our citizens.

4. Youth unemployment is a welfare issue.

5. Employment support is vital to get people back to work.

6. It is the responsibility of Government to provide a secure income for those who fall on hard times.

7. The welfare system should support families who fall on hard times and recognise the contribution they have already made through taxes and national insurance.

8. The basic need of all people is to live in community.

9. We must reject the systematic misrepresentation of the poorest in society.

10. Building self sufficiency must be a priority and welfare benefits must be used to achieve this.

Bishop Roger Sainsbury

BACKGROUND

In 1978 I wrote a Frontier Youth Trust booklet on youth unemployment, as Chair of Newham and Tower Hamlets Job Creation Committee, called 'Back on the Road to Wigan Pier'. This was followed, when I was in Walsall, in a chapter in my book 'Justice on the Agenda' called 'Unemployment and God's Creation.' In these books I shared my concerns about youth unemployment in the 1970s and 80s. Many of my concerns shared then have come up again in 2012 with one million young people unemployed. Frontier Youth Trust, the Church Urban Fund and the Churches Together in England Urban Affairs Group have been involved in a national research project involving young people in 18 neighbourhoods from Middlesbrough and Grimsby in the North East to Weston-super-Mare and Portishead in the South West. The results of this research have recently been written up in a paper – 'I am One in a Million – Young People's Experiences of Unemployment'.

The 'Youth Unemployment Ten Commandments' came from 'I am One in a Million' and an article I wrote for the Church of England Newspaper, 'Back Again on the Road to Wigan Pier? (see Appendix 5). They were shared recently at a meeting in the Frontier Youth Trust Offices in Birmingham.

Frontier Youth Trust is seeking to respond to the issues raised in 'One in a Million' by:

+ helping young people to voice their stories so that the impact of their unemployment is known and recognised

+ equipping churches to support unemployed young people

+ encouraging churches to recognise their power and influence as employers and to us it to assist young people

+ asking policy makers to ensure that those seeking work receive supportive effective assistance

We had a very positive response to the above at the seminar on youth unemployment we ran at Greenbelt 2012

YOUTH UNEMPLOYMENT TEN COMMANDMENTS

1. We need to remember our God is a Creator God and all human beings are made in His image. If young people cannot find creative work their humanity will be destroyed.

2. It is a 21st century priority to highlight the issue of youth unemployment and its effect on young people.

3. With one million young people unemployed, society must listen to the voices of young people and their experiences of being unemployed.

4. It is wrong young people should be blamed for being unemployed.

5. Government needs to recognise young people are being harder hit by the recession than other groups.

6. As churches we must recognise that if we hide our eyes from the pain of youth unemployment a whole generation of young people could reject Christianity.

7. It should be the desire of Christians to give young people purpose, direction, order and dignity that motivates them to challenge unemployment.

8. The competitive Labour Market should not result in young people being exploited by employers.

9. We must gather evidence on the impact of youth unemployment in order to exert maximum political influence to bring about specific identified change in Government policy.

10. The churches must recognise that the gravest evil and bitterest injury of the young unemployed is the spiritual grievance of being allowed no opportunity of contributing to the general life and welfare of the community.

    (N.B. Based on statement by Archbishop William Temple on unemployment in the 1930s)

    Bishop Roger Sainsbury
    President FYT and Chair CTE Urban Affairs Group
    2010 – 2012

BACKGROUND

These Ten Commandments are based on the Foreword I wrote for the Churches Together in Britain and Ireland report Asylum Voices.

Asylum and immigration have become a major domestic issue we face in the United Kingdom today. Everyone from newspaper editors to television political commentators has an opinion on people seeking asylum. But while we are forever talking about them, we do not hear their voices. Just as the report 'Faith in the City' challenged society to hear the voices of those living in poverty and deprivation, so the need to hear people seeking asylum in Britain today can no longer be ignored.

We need to address the impact of the kind of attitude that was vividly portrayed in an anonymous letter I received following my call for justice and compassion for asylum applicants, as Moderator of the Churches' Commission for Racial Justice, on the BBC Radio 4 Sunday Programme:

'Asylum seekers in the UK are confidence tricksters. They make up stories, they commit serious crimes and they support false religion. They increase house prices. If a white CofE USA person can be deported, so can all foreigners be deported.

The views of people seeking asylum and refugees themselves cannot be ignored. We need to recognize the arduous route and high personal costs involved in seeking asylum; no one does something that difficult without a compelling reason. We must engage with the human dimension of the issue, to see applicants as human beings created in the image of God, not as statistics.

In my Episcopal ministry I found many church congregations in both rural and urban areas wanted to be better informed, and surprisingly were much more generous in their judgements on people seeking asylum than sections of the press would have us believe. Action on behalf of those in need is an essential part of a living faith in Christ (James 2.14-17), and many churches continue to offer support to asylum claimants. Loving your neighbour as yourself and working for justice is at the heart of what it means to be a real Christian'.

The Rt Revd Roger Sainsbury
Moderator of CCRJ 1999 – 2003

ASYLUM AND IMMIGRATION TEN COMMANDMENTS

1. Loving your neighbour as yourself and working for justice is at the heart of what it means to be a real Christian.

2. The views of people seeking asylum and immigrants themselves cannot be ignored.

3. We need to recognise the high personal cost involved in seeking asylum.

4. We need to see applicants for asylum as human beings created in the image of God, not as statistics.

5. We must prioritize prayer for those seeking asylum and for Government to reassess policy.

6. There should be increased transparency in the process of determination of claims of people seeking asylum.

7. Detention should only be used in exceptional circumstances.

8. We need to recognise the positive cultural and economic benefits of migration.

9. We must address the root causes of forced migration.

10. We need a more humanitarian, compassionate fact-based response to the voices of immigrants and those seeking asylum.

Bishop Roger Sainsbury

BACKGROUND

At the 2011 Christian Coalition for Urban Mission Forum at Stratford, East London, called - CHAOS, DIVISIVENESS AND HOPE – one of the outcomes was that sharing a meal together can sometimes bring hope and healing to situations of divisiveness and chaos. The biblical text we focused on was Luke 15.2 'This man (Jesus) welcomes sinners (outsiders) and eats with them.' I had a letter published in the Church of England Newspaper on this theme (see below).

As a result, following the privilege of presiding at a Holy Communion Service at St. Paul's Cathedral on the 50th anniversary of my ordination as priest, Jenny and I shared Christmas dinner with the Occupy London protesters and a Biblical Quiz. The Occupy London Ten Commandments were a result the answers we received to the quiz.

LETTER CHURCH OF ENGLAND NEWS PAPER 11/11/2011

"Sir, The 2011 Urban Mission Forum in Stratford last week on 'Chaos, Divisiveness and Hope' was overshadowed by events down the road outside St. Paul's Cathedral where the protesters were camped. As some of us reflected on the question 'What would Jesus do?' a surprising biblical text emerged 'This man welcomes sinners and eats with them' (Luke 15.2). This text, we felt, perhaps gave a clue to a possible practical response to what has become a chaotic and divisive situation and be a sign of hope. As the late John Stott in his classic book 'Christ the Controversialist' points out, 'sinners' in the text is a 'scornful epithet' (pg.175) for those seen as outsiders by the religious establishment.

Some members of the Forum shared local stories about how meals had brought reconciliation and healing to their communities and others commented on the biblical fact that there are many references in the New Testament to God's Kingdom being like a feast, 'The Story of the Big Dinner' in Luke 14.15-24 being a classic one.

With the protesters now planning to be at St. Paul's Cathedral until after Christmas , a big Christmas Dinner outside St. Paul's might be an event worth considering and as one member of the Forum pointed out in Luke 15.2 it was the 'outsiders' who provided the meal for Jesus! Such a dinner might give space for genuine dialogue on neutral ground on the big biblical issues of social and economic justice, which was a major concern for Jesus and the prophets".

Bishop Roger Sainsbury CCFUM

OCCUPY LONDON TEN COMMANDMENTS

1. Seek justice, rescue the oppressed, defend the orphan, plead for the widow (Isaiah 1.12).

2. When you make a sale to your neighbour, or buy from your neighbour you shall not cheat one another (Leviticus 25.14).

3. The love of money is the root of all kinds of evil (2 Timothy 6.10).

4. Seek the welfare of the city where I have sent you (Jeremiah 29.7).

5. You who take a bribe and push the needy to the gate, seek good and not evil. (Amos 5.12-14)

6. You can not serve God and money (Luke 16.13).

7. For everything there is a season, a time to keep silent and a time to speak (Ecclesiastes 3.7).

8. Let us therefore no longer pass judgement on one another (Romans 14.13).

9. It is easier for a camel to go through the eye of a needle than for a rich man to enter the Kingdom of God (Matthew 19.24).

10. Pay all that is due to them , taxes to whom taxes are due, revenue to whom revenue is due, respect to whom respect is due (Romans 13.7).

Roger Sainsbury and Michael Eastman – CCFUM

BACKGROUND

As Chairman of the Church of England Urban Bishops' Panel I moved the 1998 Lambeth Conference Resolution on Urbanization with the introduction −'The real challenge to Christian Mission in the 21st Century will be that of urban mission (see Appendix 6). In 2008 I had retired as Bishop of Barking but as a Pastoral Tutor at Trinity College Bristol I was involved in an Evangelical Fellowship of the Anglican Communion Pre-Lambeth Urban Workshop at Trinity College. At the workshop we produced 'The Anglican Ten Commandments for Urban Mission' which were in 2010 submitted by the U.K. Urban Mission Executive (Jesus in the City) to the 2010 Edinburgh World Missionary Conference. These commandments were quoted four times in the report on that conference – 'Witnessing to Christ Today'.

I have seen the growth of cities at first hand in Asia and Africa. With a World Council of Churches delegation, I visited Pakistan and we were based in Karachi – a city which is growing every day and presenting massive problems for the nation. I visited Zambia with a Portishead Parish group and we stayed in Lusaka a city which has trebled in size in the last twenty years and is presenting a tremendous challenge to the Anglican Church there.

Chicago was the city where I was based for work on my doctorate and I saw there at first hand the need for new thinking on urban mission which I explored in my thesis- 'Preaching Faith in an Urban World.'

The major context for producing these Ten Commandments has been 42 years of ministry in East London, Liverpool and Walsall followed by ten years in Portishead which our local MP says is the fastest growing town in the U.K!

My hope would be that urban mission will be a priority for the new Archbishop, of Canterbury. Perhaps these Ten Commandments might be a guide!

ANGLICAN TEN COMMANDMENTS FOR URBAN MISSION

1. With over 50% of the world's population now living in cities, urban mission and evangelism must be a top priority for the Anglican Communion.

2. Other issues we face as Anglicans must not divert us from urban mission and evangelism as a top priority.

3. The gospel of Jesus Christ that we proclaim as Anglicans in our cities must be good news for the poor – if not, it is not the biblical gospel.

4. Seeking the welfare of our cities will involve will involve Anglicans in incarnational holistic mission.

5. Loving our neighbours as ourselves in our cities will involve Anglicans, like the Good Samaritan, crossing boundaries of faith, culture and race.

6. Mission in our cities will involve Anglicans learning to listen and give a voice to those that mainstream society wants to ignore, particularly asylum seekers.

7. Anglicans are called by God to assist in building communities of justice, equitable distribution of wealth and shalom in our cities.

8. Anglicans need to encourage the ministry of prophetic evangelism in our cities, in the tradition of the Old Testament prophets and Jesus.

9. Anglicans must repent of the sins of proclaiming a truncated, privatized gospel in our cities built on selected texts and not taking the whole of the biblical revelation seriously.

10. Anglicans are called upon to exercise a fierce commitment to staying in their urban communities, contributing to the flourishing of their cities and raising indigenous leadership.

Bishop Roger Sainsbury – UK Urban Mission Executive, 2008

BACKGROUND

These Ten Commandments came from a session at the CTE Urban Mission Group led by the Hackney Councillor Ian Rathbone and a book review I did for the Urban Bulletin on David Lammy's book 'OUT OF THE ASHES' (see Appendix 7).

While I was Chair of The National Youth Agency we produced an important report on gang culture following a National Policy Round Table which I sent to the Government Working Party that was examining the causes of the riots (see Appendix 6).

During the riots Frontier Youth Trust circulated the following prayer to its supporters:

"Father we ask for peace. Not a fluffy emotional feeling... nor a comfortable compromise... nor the wellbeing of a few... but your deep peace of SHALOM for all. We are asking for justice, wholeness, wellbeing, fairness, mercy, understanding and compassion. We pray for the victims of crime or violence and for those who have been hurt and harmed in the current troubles. We also pray against simplistic explanations of behaviour and knee jerk reactions to issues that are deep and require understanding and wisdom. We pray for those working for peace in so many guises. We remember our brothers and sisters who are involved in youth work, Street Pastoring, Street Space and a host of Christian projects around the country – both within churches and on the streets. We also remember those who work for peace in 'secular' settings: for the police, street marshals, medics, youth workers, social workers, politicians, councillors, the fire services and perhaps especially for our media. We pray for businesses and communities - that they will find a new hope and strength as they work together to recover and regain some sense of normality. We pray for the young people involved in rioting and ask that you will quicken conscience towards peaceful demonstration and dampen aggression, violence and crime. Strengthen community leaders, inspire compassion, ignite understanding and please let justice and mercy walk together in our thinking and actions. We offer these prayers through your son, our Prince of Peace, Jesus Christ. Amen."

RESPONSE TO CITY RIOTS TEN COMMANDMENTS

1. Never underestimate the cost of a riot.

2. Riots must not define communities.

3. As churches we need a clearer vision of our role – not just 'sent out' but inside the community 'building bridges'.

4. We need to start building community capacity so that young in particular have a solid base; they know they are loved, that they belong so when they do feel rejected because of lack of jobs, there is something there that gives meaning.

5. Dealing with long term youth unemployment is a priority.

6. The issues that fuel a community's mistrust of the police must be addressed.

7. Punishment and rehabilitation should be separated.

8. We need to understand the culture of gangs.

9. Young men in inner-cities need access to powerful role models.

10. Local shops and the local economy are important to the well being of the local community

Roger Sainsbury, 2011

BACKGROUND

How is faith shared in urban areas? How do people meet Jesus in their context?

How are Christian disciples formed? These and other questions were addressed in the Churches Together in England's Urban Mission Co-ordinating Group at their June 2012 meeting.

Andy Pears who works with 'UNLOCK' and 'URBAN EXPRESSION' shared his experience of incarnating God's Good News in the Easton Area of Bristol, through building relationships over many months.

CTE's report of research by John Finney published in 1992 under the title 'FINDING FAITH TODAY - HOW DOES IT HAPPEN?' is highly relevant 20 years on. Belonging precedes believing. Kinship and friendship are the key factors in the transmission of faith. Faith journeys involve a 'crystallising process' – often over several years. 'Church' has to be contextualised. Events play a part, as do life experiences. What is implicit becomes explicit, as the story of Jesus is linked with the story of the individual. His friendship is known through our friendship.

(Urban Bulletin – issue 23, 2012)
Also at our CTE meeting we shared 'TEN TIPS FOR FISHING IN URBAN AREAS' (see Appendix 9) and one of the outcomes was the 'TEN COMMANDMENTS FOR URBAN EVANGELISM' which I prepared with Jim Robertson Project Development Officer for the Churches' Regional Commission in the North-East.

URBAN EVANGELISM TEN COMMANDMENTS

1. Urban evangelism is profoundly relational.

2. Recognise and take account of the uniqueness of each social context.

3. Challenge indifference to godly perspectives.

4. Reflect on what is going on through the lived experience of the poor and ensuring their dignity.

5. Embrace dialogue and respectful engagement as essential processes.

6. Urban evangelism is prophetic and where appropriate counter cultural.

7. Urban evangelism involves, like Jesus, living alongside those who are marginalised, labelled and disadvantaged: offering an authentic witness in challenging circumstances.

8. Urban evangelism includes critically reviewing public policy through the eyes of the poor.

9. Urban evangelism may include rejecting organisations who sustain injustice and inequality.

10. Patience and endurance are essential.

Roger Sainsbury and Jim Robertson, 2012

CONCLUSION

A concern for 'Human Flourishing' was very much at the heart of the seminar we ran on youth unemployment at the 2012 Greenbelt festival.

There was also a positive response to many of the Ten Commandments in this booklet, particularly those relating to young people. In the introduction to the 2012 Greenbelt Programme Paul Northup, a Greenbelt Director says – 'Greenbelt Festival does not just entertain an audience, it galvanises a community: a raggle-taggle bunch of people who are transported and who leave wanting to LIVE, LOVE AND CREATE MORE JUSTLY, MORE GENEROUSLY'. My hope is that these Ten Commandments for Today will have the same outcome.

In the Acts of the Apostles, Stephen speaks of the Ten Commandments given to Moses as 'living oracles' (Acts 7. 38). Jesus told his disciples the purpose of His coming was that people 'may have life and have it abundantly' (John 10.10). My concern is that these Ten Commandments should not be dead letters but could in a small way be living oracles for today and enable people of all ages to live life to the full.

The Appendices that follow I hope will put flesh on the bare bones of these commandments and also show where they have come from in the rich variety of ministry I have had over the past fifty years.

APPENDIX 1

BIBLICAL TEN COMMANDMENTS

1. God said – You shall have no other god's before me.

2. You shall not make for yourself a graven image or likeness of anything that is in heaven above or earth beneath; you shall not bow down to them or serve them.

3. You shall not take the name of the Lord your God in vain.

4. Remember the Sabbath day to keep it holy. Six days you shall labour and do all your work.

5. Honour your father and mother.

6. You shall not kill

7. You shall not commit adultery

8. You shall not steal.

9. You shall not bear false witness against your neighbour

10. You shall not covet anything that is your neighbour's

APPENDIX 2

NATIONAL YOUTH AGENCY ANNUAL REPORT

2004 – 2005

THE VOICES OF YOUNG CAN MAKE A DIFFERENCE

My most exciting moment in 2005 was watching the television on July 5th when the announcement was made from Singapore that the 2012 Olympic Games were coming to London. I was excited because as a young boy I went to the 1948 Olympic Games in the old Wembley Stadium, but I was more excited when I saw a group of young people from an east London school that I had visited to take school assemblies, there in Singapore and hearing that their voices had made a difference in deciding that east London was to be the venue for the 2012 Olympic Games.

They were the same group of young people who had spoken with Nelson Mandela at 'The Make Poverty History' rally in Trafalgar Square in spring 2005. He had commented on this – 'Sometimes it falls upon a generation to be great. You can be a great generation. Let your greatness blossom.'

In my introduction to the 2005 NYA addition of *Hear by Right* I pointed out 'Young people are today's citizens. They represent an integral part of every community. We must encourage young people to express their views, to be heard and to be involved.' We sought to do that in our 2005 General Election 'Youth Manifesto' where Kierra Box, a young person and NYA Patron, in her introduction, said 'I passionately believe young people's views need to be taken into account – both about issues that directly affect them and about wider issues which may influence their future.'

One issue that young people have strong views about is the environment and climate change. I was very encouraged during a visit to speak at a major youth event in the USA when I shared the story of young people coming to The NYA Board Meeting after the 2002 UN Earth Summit, to meet young people there who were challenging their President's position on this vital issue for the future of our planet. The Secretary of State for Kentucky, who shared the platform with me, said their voices were making a difference and changing public opinion.

If the high point for me of 2005 was the decision to bring the 2012 Olympic Games to London, the low point followed two days later with the London bombings and the painful heart searching of the Muslim community. Mohammed Dhalech, the former editor of the NYA journal *Shabaab*, wrote in the summer 2005 issue of *The Edge*, 'There is a need to address the challenges that many have talked about over the last few weeks, effectively and with a clear strategy that honestly addresses the real issues.'

One of the issues Ziauddin Sardar, a Muslim author, sees, is the 'need to listen to our young men and women and pay attention to their grievances.' If there is any way that we in The National Youth Agency can facilitate this listening process we would want to make it a priority in 2006, for at the heart of our work is the belief that the voices of young people can make a difference.'

Bishop Roger Sainsbury, Chair, National Youth Agency, 2005

APPENDIX 3

FRONTIER YOUTH TRUST RESPONSERE: SERVICES FOR YOUNG PEOPLE, GOVERNMENT INQUIRY 2011

1. Thank you for the opportunity to contribute to this inquiry. FYT has been working amongst some of the most 'at risk' young people in our nation for nearly 50 years.

2. We are of the opinion that young people are the most important 'voice' in this discussion.

3. First and foremost we want to raise serious concern about the decimation of services to young people that is occurring as a result of public service cuts at this time. We are fearful of the outcomes of what we perceive to be a draconian erosion of both universal and targeted services in the youth work sector – especially in Local Authority services. Morale is at the lowest we have ever seen, youth work has become a 'depressed profession' and we are losing committed and dedicated support for young people across the whole sector. We assert that safe voluntary relationships between adults and young people within the framework of the youth work discipline [voluntary and statutory services] is crucial to young people of this nation and should be protected at all costs in these times.

4. We perceive a systemic dismantling of youth work and are most concerned given that we believe it is valuable, important and crucial aspect of community life to young people. It is especially important to those young people who are already disadvantaged and marginalised with respect to their place in society and the way that there are treated. Our own research into adult attitudes towards young people shows that young people are labelled and stigmatised in our society extensively and that this is creating a negative 'dominant narrative' that has a damaging and spiralling impact across generations. Add to intergenerational tension that is already in existence the current cuts in police and other community services and we are seriously concerned about the impact this will have across the UK.

5. We believe that any erosion of youth work services [LA and/or voluntary, targeted and/or universal] to be detrimental and short sighted in terms of the drastic impact it will have on young people. This impact will also be felt in society as a whole and upon local communities in particular. We believe that there is a distinct lack of awareness about the value of universal youth work provision that will be sharply felt if it disappears.

6. RELATIONSHIP BETWEEN UNIVERSAL AND TARGETED SERVICES

    We see the need for both, they are complimentary approaches and not competitive.

    The resources and time required to monitor targeted services is of concern to us in that it is often a complex area that takes practitioners away from face to face contact with young people and creates serious stress amongst practitioners.

    The voluntary sector is already providing a massive amount of universal services in our communities which are often used and referred to by more targeted services. We believe that not enough funding is directed towards the mobilisation, support, training, development and encouragement of existing voluntary universal services.

Dave Wiles, FYT Chief Executive, 2011

APPENDIX 4

COMMON GROUND BETWEEN CHRISTIAN AND MUSLIM YOUTH WORK

1. SPIRITUALITY ROOTED IN JUSTICE

   'Having a voice challenging discrimination and disadvantage has always been part of the youth work agenda. .For many people social justice emerges directly from their faith and spiritual framework.' This statement comes from a consultation paper prepared by The National Youth Agency at the request of the DfES. The 'many people ', two recently qualified youth workers told me at their graduation ceremony, would include both Muslim and Christian youth workers.

2. RESPECT FOR OTHERS

   'Treat your own faith with respect but also respect the faith of others' is encouraged in the NYA book 'A Sense of Respect'. A comment by Dr.Amer on chaplaincy work is also very relevant to youth work at the heart of all this, people are trying to put into practice two things, how to respect and appreciate the other.' (Faith Healing-Education Guardian 27.10.05)

3. GIVES A VOICE TO YOUNG PEOPLE

The prophet Joel spoke of a spirituality that gives a voice to young people - 'I will pour out my Spirit and your sons and your daughter shall prophesy.' Recently we have seen Christian and Muslim young peoples being heard in the 'Make Poverty History' campaign. Ziauddin Sardar comments - 'we need to listen to the voices of our young men and women' [2005 NYA Annual Report].

4. A COMMON HUMANITY

Bishop Stephen Sykes in the Church of England Doctrine Report 'Being Human' speaks of the importance of 'being human at this' time in our history'. Ziauddin Sardar comments - 'Failure makes us human. To accept you have erred and failed is a good basis on which to build the future' (Desperately Seeking Paradise). Many young people of faith and no faith have found this statement helpful. The NYA consultation paper sums up – 'spirituality is about being fully human.'

5. MAKES SPACE

Nigel Pimlott of FYT points out spiritual development of young people makes space for 'peace, depth, mystery' (Words Associated with Spirituality). Gai Eaton in the Islamic Texts Society book 'Islam and the Destiny of Man' speaks of 'Love in Mystical Experience'.

6. FAITH AS A JOURNEY

'Spiritual development for young people is about a journey of discovery' (NYA Consultation Paper). From a Muslim perspective Ziauddin Sardar comments – 'My journeys led me to one unavoidable conclusion; the Muslim paradise is not a place of arrival but a way of travelling'.

7. ROLE MODELS

Bernard Davies sees role models are very important in youth work - 'Offering the young people role models' (Youth Work Manifesto). I believe people like Martin Luther-King can provide important role models in both Muslim and Christian youth work. I once had a fascinating discussion with a young Muslim who was selling copies of the poster I HAVE A DREAM outside Ilford Station. In response to my request to buy a copy he replied -'Why do you as a Christian want to buy a poster by a good Muslim!'

8. BUILDS TRUSTING RELATIONSHIPS

'The building of trusting relationships, that is vital if we are to get over our present difficulties' (John Ray - Christians and Muslims - A view from Birmingham 2005). My time as a youth worker showed that the building of trusting relationships is at the heart of all good youth work.

9. OFFERS LOVE,SECURITY AND SIGNIFICANCE

Fred Milson, the former youth tutor at Westhill College spelt out very clearly the basic needs of all young people is for LOVE, SECURITY and SIGNIFICANCE. Young Muslims as well as young Christians have confirmed this is true for them.

10. SPIRITUALITY AND MORALITY IN NON-FORMAL EDUCATION

'A local authority shall secure shall secure, in partnership with voluntary organisations and other partners, sufficient services, facilities and programmes of non-formal education designed to promote ,through their voluntary engagement the PERSONAL, SOCIAL, MORAL, CULTURAL, SPIRITUAL, MENTAL and PHYSICAL development of young persons', (2005 NYA response to Government Green Paper). This was warmly welcomed by both Christian and Muslim youth workers.

11. BUILDS COMMUNITY COHESION

For Christians 'Loving your neighbour as yourself' is at the heart of their faith and the story Jesus told of the Good Samaritan showed very clearly love of neighbour crosses both cultural and religious divides. 'We must reach out to our neighbour not with an agenda of conversion but in simple acts of sincere love' (Muslim Community Worker in NYA 2003–04 Annual Report)

12. BOTH ENCOURAGE YOUNG PEOPLE TO EXPRESS THEIR FAITH

FYT Video: MY FAITH – CHRISTIAN AND MUSLIM YOUNG PEOPLE, a resource to help young people explore faith and life in the 21st century. Material designed to help youth workers help young people explore some of the spiritual dynamics of life in a contemporary way'.

Bishop Roger Sainsbury – Chair, NYA

APPENDIX 5

BACK AGAIN ON THE ROAD TO WIGAN PIER?

In the 1970s, when I was Warden of the Mayflower Family Centre and Chairman of Newham and Tower Hamlets Job Creation Committee, I wrote a Frontier Youth Trust booklet, *Back on the Road to Wigan Pier*, in which I shared some positive responses to a situation where, in six years, the local community of Canning Town lost 18,000 jobs. I introduced the booklet with a quote from George Orwell's book *'Road to Wigan Pier'* (1937) "lazy, idol loafers on the dole" – as many where demonising young people who were unemployed.

The positive responses I shared were three Job Creation projects the Mayflower sponsored. The first employed 25 young people to set up a farm in London Docklands – 30 years later it is still flourishing as Newham City Farm. The second was Newham Ferro-Cement Boats employing twelve young people and four adults building boats for youth and community projects – and that scheme developed into Landmark Training, now seen as one of the best youth training projects in London. The third project placed nine young people as assistants in youth and community projects. One is now the Senior Lecturer at the YMCA College, one a Social Worker and another, an Anglican Vicar.

The objective of job creation schemes was to "to prevent loss of familiarity with a working situation and help improve employment prospects". The jobs created were to be of "social value". I believe time has shown these Job Creation Projects achieved both aims,.

Every day now I have been reading of major job losses in our newspapers both nationally, where there are nearly 3 million unemployed and in Portishead the town where I now live there has been a 45 percent increase in unemployment. I am fearful again for the consequences of unemployment, particularly for young people and I am asking are we 'Back Again on the Road to Wigan Pier?'

In my 1970s booklet I explored 'Four Relevant Biblical Principles' from Genesis 1 – 3 and the prophet Amos as we sought to respond to unemployment –

1. Work is part of Natural Fabric of Society.
2. People have become Alienated from Creation.
3. People have become Excessively Possesive.
4. People Matter more than Financial Gain.

I believe these principles apply even more today as we seek as Christians to respond to the great increase in unemployment.

In the Introduction to the 1997 Church Report on 'Unemployment and the Future of Work' we read –'Underlying social justice matters are spiritual issues...despair, waste of God-given talents, contempt ,hiding the eyes from the pain of brothers and sisters.' It was because the church was seen to hide its eyes from the pain of the unemployed in George

70

Orwell's 1930s that a whole generation of men like my father, rejected Christianity. We must make sure the same thing does not happen again today.

The Prime Minister in his New Year Message has given Job Creation his highest priority. The Job Creation programmes of the 1970s enabled Christian organisations to show practical care for the unemployed, prepare them for future work and contribute in positive ways to their communities. My hope would be that the Prime Minister would be prepared to consider similar schemes today.

Bishop Roger Sainsbury – Church of England newspaper, January 2009

APPENDIX 6

GANG, GUN AND KNIFE CRIME

My first experience of gangs was in Spitalfields in the early 1960s when the Krays had a base in the Blind Beggar pub. I saw their influence on the gangs of young people who came to our church youth club. As adult role models that were encouraging young people to engage in a life of petty crime and part of our youth work was to show alternative role models.

In the late 1960s and early 70s I was engaged in full time youth work in the then notorious Scotland Road/Great Homer Street area of Liverpool. I saw how ghetto communities spawn gangs and violence. Inspired by local leaders in the community, I learnt the importance of community development and the community council that we founded still flourishes today in tackling those issues which lead young people into crime.

I then moved to be Warden of a Family Centre in Canning Town, an area of East London where a young man called Terry Smith, the author of the recent book 'The Art of Armed Robbery' lived. Terry was a leader in a gang called the 'Mini-Snipers', and a member of our youth club. During the early 80s, youth unemployment was very high in Canning Town. I was therefore fascinated by this comment in his book 'somehow we have to drag ourselves out of the gutter and adopt and embrace social and economic improvement. I chose the tools of the professional armed robber, the mask and the gun.' Our work at the Family Centre was involved in a whole variety of job creation and youth training projects which provided young people with other alternatives to the one Terry chose.

My time in Canning Town was followed by seven years in Walsall where there were ethnic and religious tensions between gangs, often associated with territory. Working with issues of racial justice and spirituality became important in one of our youth projects. These same issues were often top of the agenda when I returned to East London as Bishop of Barking. I also saw the value of good youth work and campaigned both locally and nationally for greater financial investment in youth services.

'Good youth work needs to be valued' is one of the recommendations in the report of the recent National Policy Round Table on 'GANG, GUN AND KNIFE CRIME' that I chaired. Other recommendations that make connections with the personal experience I have shared above are –

- Employment is a key path out of social exclusion and other contributing factors to gang, gun and knife crime.

- Agencies working at both a national and local level need to ensure they consult and engage with a diverse range of local community representatives.

- The issue of group crime involving weapons transcends ethnicity and occurs across all races, with neighbourhood poverty and unemployment being the underlying causes.

- While there is a clear role for enforcement and criminal justice responses to gang, gun and knife crime, prevention must feature more prominently.

Bishop Roger Sainsbury – Children and Young People Now 7–13 May, 2008

APPENDIX 7

Riots and the Banking Crisis

Urban Bulletin 2012 book review, Riots and the Banking Crisis: Out of the Ashes – David Lammy (London: Guardian Books, 2011)

Death in Florence – Paul Strathern (London: Jonathan Cape, 2011)

Two events have dominated our urban agenda during the past year: the City Riots and the Banking Crisis. These two books by David Lammy and Paul Strathern have dominated my thinking during the past year on these two events and a recent comment by Jonathan Freedland in the Guardian brought them together – ' If we were consistent, the authorities would punish the banks just as severely as they reacted to last year's riots' (30/06/2012). In his opening chapter Lammy summarized the theme of his book –'The riots were an explosion of hedonism and nihilism. People with little to lose lashed out at authority and took what they wanted. People need a proper stake in society and a much deeper sense of responsibility towards others' (p.17).

For me Chapter 7 'Banged up – Punishment versus Rehabilitation' was a key chapter in the book – 'Punishment and rehabilitation should be separated so that we can do both properly. If we understand crime as the breakdown of social trust, then punishment should serve in part to repair it' (p.172) I saw something of the truth Lammy is exploring here over 50 years ago in an Approved School in Portishead, the town where I now live.

In his final chapter Lammy comments on a fact many of us in CCFUM have been concerned about – 'unemployment remains stubbornly high' (p.234) and then makes the link with the banks and my second book –'These riots were about more than "criminality pure and simple". They were signposts to the failure of successive governments to answer the challenges of a new era of economic and social liberalism…We cannot live in a society where banks are too big to fail but whole communities are allowed to sink without trace' (p.236)

'Death in Florence' is the story of the Christian monk Savonarola who took on the banks in 15th century Florence. Strathern sees Savonarola filled with Old Testament fury and prophecies of doom but his expository biblical sermons resonated among the disenfranchised poor who were suffering from the Medici banks power in Florence. He comments – 'Banking in its modern form had to all intents and purposes been invented by the Italians' (p.17).

Savonarola has had a bad press in parts of the Christian world because of his support for burning works of art described in Chapter 17 'The Bonfire of Vanities' where Savonarola's boys are involved in 'the collecting of all manner of luxuries and ornaments that might be regarded as distracting their owners from the fundamentalist Christian way of life preached by Savonarola (p.260)

I would hope that this does not distract all Christians from the fact of the importance of Savonarola's biblical preaching in addressing the corruption of the Medici banks and his popularity with the poor of the city. The large audience for Savonarola's Lenten sermons in 1491 included all elements of the city's population but especially the poor who began to know him as the preacher for those in despair' (p.103).

In his closing chapter Strathern highlights the importance of Savonarola today in addressing a 'corrupt capitalist system run by powerful bankers'(p.370) which is 'now in the early years of the present century... a worldwide phenomenon' (p.371)

Bishop Roger Sainsbury 2012

APPENDIX 8

DEBATE ON 1998 LAMBETH CONFERENCE RESOLUTION ON URBANIZATION

Our report spells out clearly – THE REAL CHALLENGE OF TO CHRISTIAN MISSION IN THE 21ST CENTURY WILL BE THAT OF URBAN MISSION. This priority for an Anglican Communion committed to mission and evangelism has emerged in a whole variety of ways at this conference – through Section debates, through Plenaries, through Bible Studies, through Market Place events and through casual conversations with bishops from every continent. The Holy Spirit appears to be saying to the churches – URBAN MISSION IS A PRIORITY.

It is a priority firmly rooted in the scriptures where God's Story begins in a garden in Genesis and sees human destiny fulfilled in a city in Revelation. The question of John the Baptist's disciples to Jesus in the context of His city ministry – 'Are you the one who is to come or should we look for another?' Matthew 11.3 - has been a key scripture in a number of our discussions and the answer of Jesus in 11.5 about all that destroys our full humanity being challenged, the socially excluded being welcomed and the poor hearing the Good News has spelt out for us our priorities for living and proclaiming the Good News in our cities.

Urban mission is firmly part of our Anglican tradition as was shown in the Church of England report FAITH IN THE CITY which issued both a prophetic challenge in the public arena and suggested a model for urban church life which has been bearing fruit in the growth of urban churches. We have a tradition to draw on for a new millennium with different social conditions caused by increased urbanisation across the world.

We are not anti-rural for we recognise urbanization affects all communities. Our resolutions are not an example of Anglican triumphalism for we realise we need to consult and work ecumenically.

We will need to draw on the rich resources of the Anglican Communion represented at this conference – theological, experiential, social, political and financial.
If we avoid this mission challenge we could be turning a deaf ear to what the Holy Spirit has been saying to us, denying the truth of scripture and turning our backs on Anglican tradition in ways that could be disastrous.

'SEEK THE WELFARE OF THE CITY WHERE I HAVE SENT YOU – FOR IN ITS WELFARE YOU WILL FIND YOUR WELFARE'. These words of Jeremiah could be prophetic for the whole Anglican Communion as we enter the new millennium.

Bishop of Barking – City Cries Lambeth Report, November 1998

APPENDIX 9

TEN TIPS FOR FISHING IN URBAN AREAS

One of the television programmes that I have enjoyed this summer has been Channel 4's *Go Fishing*. At the same time, in my own personal Bible study, I have been looking at the opening chapters of Mark's gospel and particularly Jesus' command to his disciples, "Come with me and I will make you fishers of men" (Mark 1:17).

This issue of *City Cries*, which includes articles from some of our partners has been put together as a resource for the ECUM Urban Forum in November 1992 when we shall be looking at mission and evangelism in our cities in the Decade of Evangelism. From the *Go Fishing* programmes and the articles, I would like to suggest we can see ten tips for fishing in urban areas.

1. TAKE ACCOUNT OF THE UNIQUE ENVIRONMENT OF EACH PLACE

    Martin Wallace speaks of "an increasingly hostile environment" for evangelism today, particularly in the inner city.

2. NEED FOR LOCAL GUIDES

Jenny Richardson comments on the importance of 'sitting alongside the indigenous' and Margaret Owen on giving 'time and space for local people to talk'.

3. GETTING OUT OF THE BOAT

Michael Eastman challenges the church to 'go to the clubs, pubs, discos, shopping centres, leisure parks and street corners' and to work with 'young offenders, AIDS sufferers, young homeless and young unemployed'.

4. OLD EXPERTS NEED TO LEARN NEW THINGS

Peter Hobson speaks of the problem of 'the older worthies' in urban mission and James Ashdown of 'the increasing complexity of the city' and the need for training.

5. READING UP OTHER PEOPLE'S EXPERIENCES CAN BE HELPFUL

City Cries book reviews can help us to widen our nets and increase our vision.

6. PARTNERSHIP WITH OTHERS

Basil Scott talks of the need for 'multi-racial teams, combining different gifts, in partnership with one or more churches'.

7. IMPORTANCE OF SURVEYING THE SCENE

Michael Eastman quotes from a number of surveys of homelessness, unemployment, drug addiction etc. These surveys are important in preparation for evangelism.

8. PATIENCE AND ENDURANCE ARE ESSENTIAL

Jenny Richardson speaks of the importance of 'quietly working for justice' and 'encouraging each other to confidently go on'.

9. BE PREPARED FOR DISAPPOINTMENTS

Most of us can identify with the title of FYT's 1993 conference, *I came, I saw, I struggled.*

10. ENJOY IT!

James Ashdown talks of 'the joys of London life'. If we go fishing we need to enjoy it, and for effective evangelism we need both to share the pain and enjoy the life of our cities

Bishop Roger Sainsbury – City Cries, November 1992

BIBLIOGRAPHY

Percy, M., (2011) *Reflections for Daily Prayer*, Church House Publishing: London

Atkinson M., (2012) August edition. NAME OF ARTICLE Children and Young People Now: London

De Botton A., (2011) *Religion for Atheists*, Penguin: London

Sainsbury R., (1970) *From a Mersey Wall*, Scripture Union: London

Pimlott J. & N., (2008) *Youth Work after Christendom*, Paternoster: London

JPTI Report, (2013) *The Lies We Tell Ourselves*

Smith T., (DATE) *The Art of Armed Robbery*, John Blake Publishing: LOCATION

Brueggeman W., (DATE) *Jeremiah*, Hansel Press: Edinburgh

Sainsbury, R., (2003) *Asylum Voices*, Churches Together in Britain and Ireland: London

Stott, J., (1970) *Christ the Controversialist*, Tyndale Press: London

Balia, D. & Kim K., (2010) *Witnessing to Christ Today Edinburgh 2010*, Vol.2, Regnum Books: Oxford

Lammy, D., (2011) *Out of the Ashes*, Guardian Books: London

Strathern, P., (2011) *Death in Florence,* Jonathan Cape: London

Finney, J,. (1992) *Finding Faith Today,* CTE: London

USEFUL ADDRESSES

PORTISHEAD YOUTH CENTRE
Harbour Road, PORTISHEAD BS20 7DD

FRONTIER YOUTH TRUST
St. George's Community Hub, Great Hampton Row, Newton, BIRMINGHAM B19 3JG

THE NATIONAL YOUTH AGENCY
Eastgate House, 19-23 Humberstone Road, LEICESTER LE5 3GJ

THE CENTRE FOR YOUTH MINISTRY
Trinity Business Centre, Stonehill Green, SWINDON SN5 7DG

CHRISTIAN COALITION FOR URBAN MISSION
Bethnal Green Mission Church, 305 Cambridge Heath Road, LONDON E2 9LH

CHURCHES TOGETHER IN ENGLAND URBAN GROUP
27 Tavistock Square, LONDON WC1H 9HH

UK URBAN MISSION CONGRESS TRUST
Union Theological College, 108 Botanic Avenue, BELFAST B171JT

TRINITY COLLEGE
Stoke Hill, BRISTOL BS9 1JP

SHREWSBURY HOUSE
37 Langrove Street, Everton, LIVERPOOL L5 3PE

GREENBELT FESTIVALS
83 London Wall, LONDON EC2M 5ND